Math Practice Questions

1. A club has 34 members, and 18 of them are new. If two new members quit the club, what percentage of the remaining people in the club are not new members?
   a. 6%
   b. 47%
   c. 50%
   d. 53%
   e. 59%

2. A rare book has increased in value by 35% over the past six months. If the book is worth $340.00 today, what was the value six months ago?
   a. $119.00
   b. $204.20
   c. $240.00
   d. $251.90
   e. $305.00

3. Jacob needs an average of 120 points or above over six games to qualify for the finals round in a tournament. His average score in the first five games was 117 points. What minimum score does he need to qualify?
   a. 117
   b. 120
   c. 132
   d. 135
   e. 138

4. The average of j and k is 22, and the average of k and m is 17. If k equals 20, what is the average of j and m?
   a. 19
   b. 19.5
   c. 21
   d. 22
   e. 22.5

5. The median of a set of numbers is smaller than the average of the same set. If the average is 15, which of the following MUST be true of the set?

I. More than half of the numbers in the set are smaller than 15

II. The greatest number in the set is at least twice as large as the average

III. The range of the set is at least 15

a. I only

b. I and II

c. II only

d. I and III

e. II and III

6. Which of the following is equal to : $\sqrt[3]{x^2 y^6}$?

a. $\dfrac{y^3}{x}$

b. $\sqrt[2]{x^3 y^6}$

c. $x^{\frac{3}{2}} y^2$

d. $x * x * y * y * y * y$

e. $x^{\frac{2}{3}} * y * y$

7. The Least Common Multiple of two numbers is 45. Which of the following pairs of numbers fits this description?

a. 3 and 5

b. 5 and 9

c. 3 and 15

d. 5 and 15

e. 9 and 15

8. Gillian and Sasha are running in a relay race. First, Gillian runs 200 meters, and then she tags Sasha, who runs the next 200 meters. Gillian's speed is 250 meters per minute. If the team finishes the relay in 2.4 minutes, what is Sasha's speed?

a. 100 meters per minute

b. 125 meters per minute

c. 150 meters per minute

d. 175 meters per minute

e. 200 meters per minute

9. This year, the number of subscribers to an online journal is twice the number of subscribers from last year. Last year, there were three times as many subscribers as the year before that. If there were 87 subscribers two years ago, how many subscribers are there this year?

    a. 174
    b. 261
    c. 522
    d. 687
    e. 783

10. Which of the following is the Greatest Common Factor of 68, 102, and 170?

    a. 4
    b. 6
    c. 17
    d. 32
    e. 68

11. If y is a negative number and the value of $\dfrac{y^3}{4}$ equals the value of $\dfrac{y^5}{4}$, which is a possible value for , which is a possible value for y?

    a. −2
    b. −1
    c. 0
    d. 1
    e. 2

12. In the figure below, one side of regular pentagon ABCDE lies along line DG. What is the value of x?

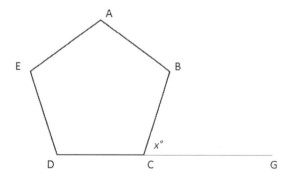

    a. 42
    b. 55
    c. 72
    d. 84
    e. 108

13. In the figure below, Line DEF passes through the center O of the circle. If E lies at the midpoint of the line and the length of DEF is 32, what is the area of the circle?

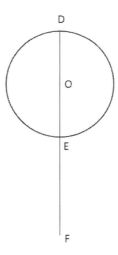

    a. 8π
    b. 16π
    c. 32π
    d. 48π
    e. 64π

14. In the figure below, JK lies parallel to LM. LQ is perpendicular to NP. If angle QLM is 37°, what is the size of angle PRK?

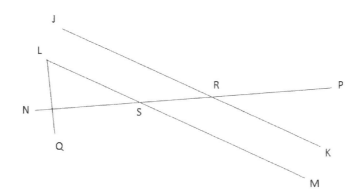

    a. 37°
    b. 43°
    c. 53°
    d. 67°
    e. 127°

15. A number squared is equal to that number times three. Which of the following could not be the number?
   a. −1
   b. 1
   c. 0
   d. 3
   e. All of the above could be the number.

16. If $y = 7x + 3$, what is the range of y values when $-5 \leq x \leq 5$?
   a. $32 \leq y \leq 38$
   b. $-32 \leq y \leq 38$
   c. $-32 \geq y \geq 38$
   d. $-38 \geq y \geq 32$
   e. $-38 \leq y \leq 32$

17. Every day, four of the flights leaving a small airport go to Chicago. There are six flights scheduled to leave the airport one morning and three flights scheduled to leave that afternoon. If one of the afternoon flights is going to Chicago, what is the probability that any one morning flight is going to Chicago?
   a. 25%
   b. 33%
   c. 50%
   d. 66%
   e. 75%

18. A recipe calls for 1/3 cup of chopped onions to make six servings. If the recipe needs to be scaled to make 45 servings, how many cups of chopped onions are needed?
   a. 1/3
   b. 1
   c. 1.5
   d. 2 and 1/3
   e. 2.5

19. Based on the portion of the graph shown below, for which value of x is $f(x) = g(x)$?

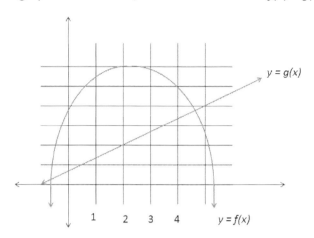

a. −2

b. 0

c. 2

d. 3.5

e. 4.5

20. $4x^2 = 36$. What is the value of $\dfrac{x^4}{9}$?

a. 3

b. 9

c. 18

d. 72

e. 81

21. Triangles ABC and DEF are similar. A, D, C, and F are collinear. What is the value of x?

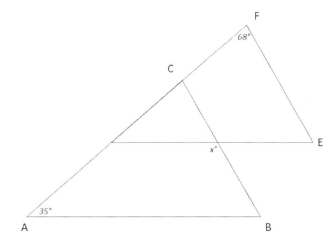

a. 35

7

b. 55

c. 77

d. 103

e. 112

22. A non-hollow sphere is fitted inside of a cube so that it touches each side of the cube at one point. Which of the following expresses the ratio of the volume of the cube that is not taken up by the sphere?

    a. $1 - \pi/6$

    b. $\pi/3$

    c. $1 - 2\pi/3$

    d. $1 - \pi^2/3$

    e. $\pi^2/8$

23. For what value of y does the graph of $2y = 8 - 15x$ intercept the x-axis?

    a. -15

    b. $-15/2$

    c. 0

    d. 4

    e. 8

24. Which of the following expressions is equal to $\dfrac{k^2 m^3}{2k^8 m^2}$?

    a. $\dfrac{k^{\frac{1}{6}} m}{2}$

    b. $\dfrac{m}{2k^6}$

    c. $\dfrac{2m}{k^6}$

    d. $\dfrac{k^{-6} m^{-1}}{2}$

    e. $\dfrac{k^{-6}}{2m}$

25. A sequence of numbers begins with: 2, 3, 8, 63. What is the next number in the sequence?

    a. 3968

    b. 3905

    c. 3842

    d. 3779

    e. None of the Above

26. Eight more than half of a number is equal to 56. What is that number?

    a. 108

b. 120

c. 84

d. 96

e. 82

27. If $|x - 7| > 4$, what is one possible value of x?

    a. x<7

    b. x>11 or x<3

    c. x=11

    d. x<14 or x>11

    e. x>14 or x>3

28. $5(x - y) + z = 540$

    $2x + 4y - 2z = 360$

    Given the system of equations above, what is the value of $2x - y$?

    a. 200

    b. 96

    c. 240

    d. 320

    e. 340

29. The value of a car is 60% less than it was four years ago. If the car is now worth $2400, what was the value of the car four years ago?

    a. $3,200

    b. $4,400

    c. $4,000

    d. $6,000

    e. $6,600

30. What is the product of the first prime number that is greater than 60 and the smallest positive prime number?

    a. 122

    b. 84

    c. 136

    d. 140

    e. 131

31. A shaved ice stand sells a snow-cone for $1.50. If the materials for each snow-cone cost $0.25, and the cost to run the stand is $120 per day, how many snow-cones need to be sold in five days for the stand to make a profit of $500?

    a. 700

    b. 880

    c. 780

d. 800

e. 920

32. If $\frac{2m}{n}$ = 9 and $n = 3$, what is the value of $\frac{m}{2}$?

    a. 5.75
    b. 3.45
    c. 6.75
    d. 8.25
    e. 7.25

33. A tile pattern is made of regular octagons and squares, as shown:

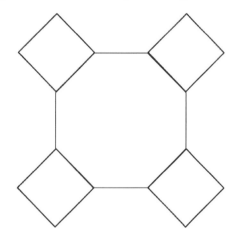

If the perimeter of one of these squares is 12 centimeters, what is the area in square centimeters, rounded to the nearest square centimeter, of the pattern segment shown?
    a. 132 cm^2
    b. 141 cm^2
    c. 156 cm^2
    d. 159 cm^2
    e. 165 cm^2

34. A number p can be completely factored as 2*3*5*m*m. If p = 5070, what is the value of m?
    a. 15
    b. 14
    c. 12
    d. 17
    e. 13

35. Two lines have the equations:

$$1.5x+4y = 8$$
$$-3y + 9x = 9$$

Which of the following statements about the lines are true?

    I.   The lines have the same y-intercept

    II.   The lines never intersect

    III.   The lines intersect in the third quadrant

    a. I only

    b. II and II

    c. III only

    d. I and III

    e. None of the statements are true.

36. The shortest distance between the points (4, k) and (11, 2k) can be expressed as:

    a. $\sqrt{(k + 7)(k - 7)}$

    b. $k^2 + 49$

    c. $\sqrt{15^2 + 9k^2}$

    d. $k^2 - 49$

    e. $\sqrt{(4 - k)^2 + (11 - 2k)^2}$

37. A clothing store sells four different brands of sandals. Two of the brands come in children's and adults' sizes, and three of the brands sell waterproof sandals. If two brands sell only waterproof adults' sandals, how many brands sell waterproof children's sandals?

    a. 0

    b. 1

    c. 2

    d. 3

    e. 4

38. A design for a banner includes a striped background. The stripes are colored in the repeating order: yellow, blue, orange, green, and purple. What color is the 37th stripe?

a. yellow

b. blue

c. orange

d. green

e. purple

Questions 39 – 41 use the information below:

The following table gives information for rainfall over a six-month period:

Month	Rainfall (inches)
June	2.1
July	0.6
August	1.4
September	x
October	y
November	4.2

39. If the average rainfall over the six-month period was 2.3 inches per month, what was the total rainfall in September?

    a. 2.1

    b. 2.3

    c. 3.0

    d. 3.2

    e. Cannot be determined from the information given

40. If the average rainfall over the six-month period was 1.7 inches per month, what was the total rainfall from September 1 through October 31?

    a. 1.7

    b. 1.9

    c. 3.4

    d. 8.3

    e. Cannot be determined from the information given

41. The total rainfall for this area in November has grown 20% from the year before. What was the total rainfall in November for the year before the one shown?

    a. 0.8

    b. 2.4

    c. 3.5

    d. 4.2

    e. 5.0

42. A rectangular lot is divided by a fence as shown:

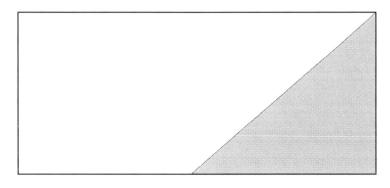

6 meters

14 meters

The fence bisects the bottom edge of the rectangle. What percent of the lot is shaded?
   a. 25%
   b. 28%
   c. 30%
   d. 33%
   e. 43%

43. Line a intersects line b, forming angles of 135° and 45°. A third line, line c, is perpendicular to line a and forms triangle ABC. What is the measure of the angle between lines b and c?
   a. 35°
   b. 45°
   c. 90°
   d. 135°
   e. The answer cannot be determined from the information given.

44. Alexei has a pencil bag containing one of more of each of the following: red pens, blue pens, mechanical pencils, and black markers. He knows that there is a 4% chance he will pull a red pen out of the bag if he chooses randomly. What is the number of total pens, pencils, and markers in the bag?
   a. 15
   b. 20
   c. 25
   d. 40
   e. 60

13

45. A rectangle has a perimeter of 140 feet. The length of the rectangle is three times its width. Which is the closest, in square feet, to the area of the rectangle?
    a. 900
    b. 1000
    c. 1100
    d. 1200
    e. 1400

46. A record plays with a speed of 33 1/3 revolutions per minute, meaning that a needle in a groove around the edge of the record will make 33 and 1/3 circuits around the record in one minute. If the diameter of the record is 40 centimeters, how many centimeters does the needle travel in one minute?
    a. 400
    b. 1333 1/3
    c. 2000
    d. 2400
    e. 2666 2/3

47. The expression $\frac{1.55 * 10^7}{9.22 * 10^{-3}}$ is nearest to which of the following?
    a. Ten thousand
    b. One million
    c. Ten million
    d. One billion
    e. Ten billion

48. A line with a slope of -2 passes through the point (8,0). What is the set of coordinates when that line passes through the *y*-axis?

    a. (8, 0)
    b. (0, −8)
    c. (0, 16)
    d. (−16, 0)
    e. (0, −16)

49. Use the following functions to answer the question:
$$f(x) = x^3 + 1$$

$$g(x) = 4(x - 1)$$

What is the value of $f(g(\frac{3}{2}))$?

    a. 35/8
    b. 9
    c. 2
    d. 27/2
    e. 7

50. A taco stand sells tacos with any three ingredients for a flat price of $1.25. Additional ingredients cost $0.50 each. There are ten different possible ingredients. How many different types of tacos costing $2.25 can be made at the stand?
    a. 160
    b. 252
    c. 345
    d. 452
    e. 610

Questions 50 – 55 cover trigonometry concepts, which are only tested on the ACT.

Questions 51 and 52 use the figure below:

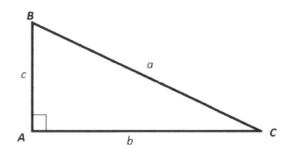

51. Which of the following is equivalent to the value of the tangent of angle C?

    a. $\dfrac{c}{a}$

    b. $\dfrac{a}{c}$

    c. $\dfrac{c}{b}$

    d. $\dfrac{b}{c}$

    e. 1

52. If angle B has a measure of 38° and line segment *a* has an approximate length of 10 inches, what is the approximate length in inches of line segment *c*?

    a. 6.2

    b. 6.8

    c. 7.4

    d. 7.9

    e. 12.8

53. The graph below is a graph of which equation?

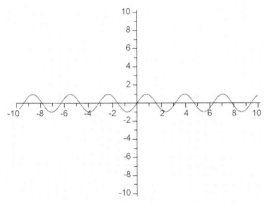

    a. $f(x) = 2sin(x)$
    b. $f(x) = cos(2x)$
    c. $f(x) = 2cos(x)$
    d. $f(x) = sin(2x)$
    e. $f(x) = 2tan(x)$

Questions 54 and 55 use the diagram below:

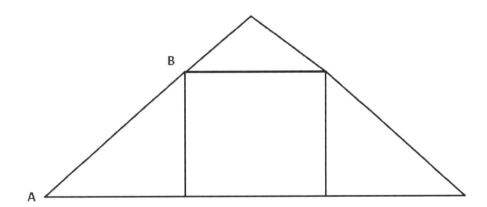

The roof truss shown is one large isosceles triangle braced by the square in the center.

54. If the length of the roof is 15 feet across the base and the height is 7 feet at the highest point, what is the angle measure at each corner (the pitch of the roof)?
    a. 21°
    b. 38°
    c. 43°
    d. 55°
    e. 69°

55. The base of the square is the same length as the bases of the two smaller triangles on either side of the truss shown. What is the length of hypotenuse AB?
    a. $5\sqrt{2}$
    b. 5
    c. $2\sqrt{2}$
    d. $5\sqrt{5}$
    e. 7

Math Practice Answers

Question	Answer	Question	Answer	Question	Answer	Question	Answer
1	C	11	B	21	D	31	B
2	D	12	C	22	A	32	C
3	D	13	E	23	C	33	D
4	A	14	C	24	B	34	E
5	A	15	A	25	A	35	E
6	E	16	B	26	D	36	A
7	E	17	C	27	B	37	B
8	B	18	E	28	C	38	B
9	C	19	E	29	D	39	E
10	D	20	B	30	A	40	B

Question	Answer	Question	Answer
41	C	51	C
42	A	52	D
43	B	53	D
44	C	54	C
45	A	55	A
46	B		
47	D		
48	E		
49	B		
50	B		

Math Solutions

1. Step 1: $34 - 18 = 16$ (number of old members)
   Step 2: $34 - 2 = 32$ (number of total members after two leave)
   Step 3: $16/32 = .5$, which is 50%

2. Step 1: $1 + .35 = 1.35$ (percentage increase)
   Step 2: $1.35x = 340$ (set up the equation)
   Step 3: $x = 251.9$ (original value)

3. Step 1: $117 * 5 = 585$ (total points scored so far)
   Step 2: $120 * 6 = 720$ (total points needed)
   Step 3: $720 - 585 = 135$ (score needed in the last game)

4. Step 1: $(j + 20)/2 = 22$, so $j = 24$
   Step 2: $(20 + m)/2 = 17$, so $m = 14$
   Step 3: $(24 + 14)/2 = 19$

8. Step 1: 200 meters = 250 meters per minute $* t$, so $t = .8$ minutes (finding Gillian's time)
   Step 2: 200 meters = Rate $* (2.4 - 0.8)$, so Rate = 125 (finding Sasha's rate)

9. Step 1: $87 * 3 = 261$
   Step 2: $261 * 2 = 522$

12. Step 1: $(5 - 2) * 180 = 540$ (total number of degrees inside the pentagon)
    Step 2: $540/5 = 108$ (size of each interior angle)
    Step 3: $180 - 108 = 72$ (value of x)

13. Step 1: $32/2 = 16$ (length of DE)
    Step 2: $16/2 = 8$ (radius of the circle)
    Step 3: $\pi(8)^2 = 64\pi$

14. Step 1: $180 - 90 - 37 = 53$ (measure of angle LSN)
    Step 2: Since LM is parallel to JK, LSN and PRK are similar angles.

16. Step 1: $y = 7(-5) + 3 = -32$
    Step 2: $y = 7(5) + 3 = 38$

17. Step 1: $4 - 1 = 3$ (number of flights for Chicago in the morning)
    Step 2: $3/6 = .5$ (probability of a morning flight going to Chicago)

18. Step 1: $\dfrac{\frac{1}{3}}{6} = \dfrac{x}{45}$ (set up a ratio; there are several correct ways to set up)

    Step 2: x = 2.5

20. Step 1: $x^2 = 9$, so x = 3

    Step 2: $3^4/9 = 9$

21. Step 1: $180 - 35 - 68 = 77$ (35 and 68 are the similar angle measures in the smaller triangle)

    Step 2: $180 - 77 = 103$ (measure of x)

22. Step 1: Volume of the cube: L*W*H

    Step 2: Volume of the sphere: $4/3(\pi r^2)$

    Step 3: Substitute "2r" for length, width, and height of cube

    Step 4: Expression for the area not filled by sphere over the total area of the cube:

$$\dfrac{(2r)^3 - \frac{4}{3}\pi r^3}{(2r)^3}$$

    Step 5: Reduce.

23. All graphs intercept the x-axis when $y = 0$

25. The pattern is to square the previous number and subtract one.

26. $(x/2) + 8 = 56$; x = 96

27. Step 1: $x - 7 < -4$, so x < 3

    Step 2: $x - 7 > 4$, so x > 11

28. Step 1: Multiply first equation by 2: $10x - 10y + 2z = 1080$

    Step 2: Add equations: $12x - 6y = 1440$

    Step 3: Reduce: $2x - y = 240$

29. Step 1: $2400 = (1 - 0.6)x$

    Step 2: x = 6000

30. Step 1: $61 * 2 = 122$

31. Step 1: $\$500 = (1.5 - 0.25)x - (120 * 5)$

    Step 2: $1100 = 1.25x$; x = 880

32. Step 1: $\dfrac{2m}{3} = 9$, so m = 13.5

    Step 2: m/2 = 6.75, or 27/4

33. Step 1: If the perimeter of the square is 12, one side is 3 cm long. Area of each square = 9 cm^2

    Step 2: Area of the octagon: there are several ways to figure this out. One is to fill in the edges of the octagon to make a larger square, noticing that the four corners added are the size of one of the small squares in the pattern. The larger square we've made has side length of $3 + 2(3\sqrt{2})$, which equals approximately 11.5. Area of the larger square would then be 131.9. Subtract the area of one triangle to get the area of the octagon: $131.9 - 9 = 122.9$

    Step 3: Area of the whole pattern = $122.9 + 4(9)$ is approximately 159 cm^2

34. Step 1: $2*3*5*m*m = 5040$, so m = 13

36. Step 1: Distance formula: $\sqrt{(2k - k)^2 + (11 - 4)^2}$

    Step 2: Reduce: $\sqrt{(k)^2 + (7)^2}$

    Step 3: Factor: $\sqrt{(k + 7)(k - 7)}$

38. Step 1: Since the pattern has five components, divide 37/5 = 7 remainder 2

    Step 2: The color is the number of the remainder, so the second one in the pattern: blue.

40. Step 1: $(1.7)*6 = 10.2$ (Total rainfall over six months)

    Step 2: $10.2 - 2.1 - 0.6 - 1.4 - 4.2 = 1.9$ (total rainfall in Sept and Oct)

41. Step 1: $4.2 = (1 + .2)x$

42. Step 1: Area of the total rectangle = $6*14 = 84$ square meters

    Step 2: Area of the triangle = $\frac{1}{2} * 7 * 6 = 21$ square meters (we know the base is 7 meters since it is half of the bisected 14 meters)

    Step 3: $21/84 * 100 = 25\%$

43. The triangle must have angles of 90, 45, and 45 degrees.

44. Step 1: $1/x = .04$, therefore x = 25 total pens and pencils and markers.

45. Step 1: $2L + 2W = 140$ (perimeter equation)

    Step 2: L = 3W

    Step 3: Substitute: 6W + 2W = 140; W = 17.5 feet.

    Step 4: Find L = 52.5 feet

    Step 5: Find the area: $17.5 * 52.5 = 918.75$ square feet

46. Step 1: rate = distance * time

    Step 2: 1 revolution = 40 cm

    Step 3: (40 cm)(33 1/3 revolutions)/minute = distance * 1 minute

    Step 4: 1333 1/3 cm = distance

47. $10^7/10^{-3} = 10^{10}$ = One billion

48. Step 1: slope = $\frac{y2-y1}{x2-x1}$

    Step 2: -2 = $\frac{y2-0}{8-0}$, so y_2 = -16

49. Step 1: g(3/2) = 4(3/2 − 1) = 2

    Step 2: f(2) = 2^3 + 1 = 9

50. Step 1: 2.25 = 1.25 + .5x, x = 2. Therefore the taco has five ingredients (3+2)

    Step 2: Combination problem, since order does not matter: 10!/(5!*5!) = 252

51. Step 1: tanC = b/c

52. Step 2: cos(38) = c/10; c = 7.9

53. Step 1: Does the graph pass through the origin? Yes – sin, not cos.

    Step 2: Is the graph elongated along the x-axis or y-axis? X-axis – it's sin(2x).

54. Step 1: Cut the roof in half to make a right triangle with a height of 7 feet and a base of 7.5 feet.

    Step 2: tan(angle) = 7/7.5

    Step 3: angle = 43°

55. Step 1: Find the base of the square and triangle: 15/3 = 5

    Step 2: All sides of the square must be 5 feet, so the two sides of the left triangle are 5 feet as well.

    Step 3: Hypotenuse = $\sqrt{5^2 + 5^2}$ = $5\sqrt{2}$

Reading/English/Language Arts

The following sentences contain either one error or no errors. For questions 1 through 10, select the underlined section that contains the error, or select "E" for "no error."

1. <u>Having</u> a fire safety plan so that <u>each member</u> of the household knows <u>at least two ways</u> to exit the house, how to avoid smoke inhalation, and where to meet up with the other household members <u>once</u> outside.
   A. Having
   B. each member
   C. at least two ways
   D. once
   E. No error

2. The longest filibuster <u>ever</u> completed in the United States Senate <u>lasted for</u> twenty four hours and eighteen minutes and <u>was</u> conducted by Strom Thurmond, <u>a Senator from South Carolina</u>.
   A. ever
   B. lasted for
   C. was
   D. a Senator from South Carolina
   E. No error

3. <u>Everybody</u> in the class <u>knew</u> that the only way we <u>would be able to</u> complete the presentations on time was if we each <u>refrain from</u> asking too many questions.
   A. Everybody
   B. knew
   C. would be able to
   D. refrain from
   E. No error

4. Each of the following rules <u>are critical</u> for <u>maintaining</u> a functioning organization: all members must be present for votes, <u>processes are</u> recorded in writing, and <u>nobody</u> can take all the credit for any one decision.
   A. are critical
   B. maintaining
   C. processes are
   D. nobody
   E. No error

5. Ruby <u>knew</u> when she invited <u>Emma and me</u> over for dinner that <u>there would</u> be <u>a lot</u> of extra food.
- A. knew
- B. Emma and me
- C. there would
- D. a lot
- E. No error

6. <u>It is well</u> understood <u>by</u> chemists that adding heat to <u>systems make</u> reactions happen <u>more quickly</u>.
- A. It is well
- B. by
- C. systems make
- D. more quickly
- E. No error

7. Even though <u>we all know</u> that the best way to prevent <u>spreading</u> germs is to wash our hands often and <u>properly,</u> many people <u>failed</u> to do it.
- A. we all know
- B. spreading
- C. properly
- D. failed
- E. No error

8. Big Bend National Park, the Grand Canyon, and Carlsbad Caverns – <u>each</u> of these places <u>have been</u> described <u>as treasures</u> <u>of the</u> American Southwest.
- A. each
- B. have been
- C. as treasures
- D. of the
- E. No error

9. To help <u>students</u> find books <u>on</u> <u>which</u> they will truly be engaged <u>is</u> the main goal of any school librarian.
- A. students
- B. on
- C. which
- D. is
- E. No error

10. Every summer, this city <u>benefits from</u> the arts festival: travelers <u>spend</u> money at the local hotels and restaurants, news outlets <u>bring</u> attention to the town, and local citizens <u>having</u> lots of fun.
    A. benefits from
    B. spend
    C. bring
    D. having
    E. No error

In the passages that follow, certain words and phrases are underlined, and the sentences with those underlined sections are numbered. Each passage is followed by questions about the underlined sections. Each question has five answer choices. If NO CHANGE is given as an answer choice, you can select that when you think that the original underlined section in the passage is better than the alternatives listed as the other answer choices. Some questions are not about specific underlined portions, but the passage as a whole.

Passage 1: Analyzing People

This passage is excerpted from *How to Analyze People on Sight through the Science of Human Analysis*, a text published in 1921 by Elsie Lincoln Benedict, which is in the public domain. The passage has been altered for the purposes of the test. Questions 11 – 20 refer to this passage.

The most essential thing in the world <u>to any individual is to understand themselves</u> (1). The next is to understand everyone else (2). Life is largely a problem of running your own car as it was built to be run, <u>also to get along with the other drivers on the highway</u> (3). You must learn which type of car you are and the main reasons why you <u>have not got</u> the best mileage out of yourself (4). Also, you must learn the makes of other human cars, and how to be getting the maximum cooperation out of them (5). We come in contact with our fellow man in all the activities of our lives and what we get out of life depends, to an astounding degree, <u>on our relations with him</u> (6).

<u>So long as you live in a thickly populated community you will need to understand your own nature and the natures of other people</u> (7). No matter what you desire from life, other people's aims, ambitions and activities constitute vital obstructions along your pathway (8). You will never get far without the cooperation, confidence and comradeship of other men and women (9). The work of thousands of human hands and <u>thousands of human brains lie behind</u> every meal you eat, every journey you take, every book you read, every bed in which you sleep, every telephone conversation, and every garment you wear (10).

11. The best version of the underlined portion of Sentence (1) is:
    A. NO CHANGE
    B. to all individuals is to understand themselves
    C. to any individual is to understand his or herself
    D. is to understand themselves
    E. is for individuals to understand themselves

12. The author would like to combine sentences (1) and (2). Which of the following would be the best method to do so?
    A. The most essential thing in the world to any individual is to understand themselves and the next most essential thing is to understand everyone else.
    B. The most essential thing in the world to any individual is to understand themselves; and the next is to understand everyone else.
    C. The most essential thing in the world to any individual is to understand themselves but the next is to understand everyone else.
    D. The most essential thing in the world to any individual is to understand themselves and then the next is to understand everyone else.
    E. The most essential thing in the world to any individual is to understand themselves; the next is to understand everyone else.

13. The best version of the underlined portion of Sentence (3) is:
    A. NO CHANGE
    B. also getting along with the other drivers on the highway
    C. and to get along with the other drivers on the highway
    D. and getting along with the other drivers on the highway
    E. getting along with the other drivers on the highway

14. The best version of the underlined portion of Sentence (4) is:
    A. NO CHANGE
    B. haven't getting
    C. have got
    D. have not been getting
    E. have not get

15. The best version of the underlined portion of Sentence (5) is:
    A. NO CHANGE
    B. how to be getting the maximum cooperation out of him

28

C. getting the maximum cooperation out of them

D. how to be getting the maximum of cooperation out of them

E. how to get the maximum cooperation out of them

16. The best version of the underlined portion of Sentence (6) is:

    A. NO CHANGE

    B. on our relations with them

    C. in our relations with him

    D. in our relations with them

    E. upon our relations with him

17. Sentences (8) and (9) directly support which sentence?

    A. 1

    B. 4

    C. 6

    D. 7

    E. 10

18. The best version of Sentence (7) is:

    A. NO CHANGE

    B. As long as you live in a thickly populated community you will need to understand your own nature and the natures of other people.

    C. As long as you live in a thickly populated community you will need to understand your own nature and those of other people.

    D. So long as you live in a thickly populated community you will need to understand your own nature and those of other people.

    E. As long as you are living in a thickly populated community you will need to understand your own nature and those of other people.

19. The author would like to add the following sentence into the passage: "Today we depend for life's necessities almost wholly upon the activities of others." After which sentence is this new sentence best placed?

    A. 5

    B. 6

    C. 7

    D. 8

    E. 9

20. The best version of the underlined portion of Sentence (10) is:

A. NO CHANGE
B. a thousand human brains lie behind
C. thousands of human brains lies behind
D. thousands of human brains are lying behind
E. a thousand human brains are lying behind

Passage 2: The Bathyscaphe

This passage is original to this test. Questions 21 – 34 refer to this passage.

For as long as we've been able to, humans have explored <u>the most far reaches</u> of the natural world (1). From the tops of mountain peaks, to the polar ice caps on both ends of the planet, even out into space, we <u>attempted</u> to learn more about our place on the planet and in the universe (2). Second only to space exploration is the deep sea (3). Apart from the epipelagic layer of the ocean, which is the top layer, the sea is <u>terrible inhospitable to human exploration</u> (4). The pressure in the ocean increases by one atmosphere <u>every ten meters deeper</u> – one atmosphere is the pressure experienced on land at sea level, so twenty meters into the ocean, the pressure is three times what you feel on land (5)! Not to mention the darkness and extreme cold in the deeper layers of the sea (6).

Remarkably, humans descended to the deepest part of the ocean in 1960, <u>the same decade that humans landed on the Moon</u> (7). This was done by an international research team that <u>designed, built, and piloting the bathyscaphe <i>Trieste</i></u> (8). A bathyscaphe is a submersible sea vessel <u>designed to withstand the intensity of pressure</u> found in the deeper layers of the ocean (9). The <i>Trieste</i> went all the way to the ocean floor in the Challenger Deep, <u>which is the deepest known point of the ocean, having a depth around 11,000 meters deep</u> (10). <u>They were able to use high-powered lights</u> down there to discover the existence of biological life in the deepest known place on Earth (11).

21. The best version of the underlined portion of Sentence (1) is:
    A. NO CHANGE
    B. the farthest reaches
    C. reaches most far
    D. far reaches
    E. reaching far

22. The best version of the underlined portion of Sentence (2) is:
    A. NO CHANGE
    B. attempt
    C. were attempting
    D. have attempted
    E. are attempting

23. Which is the best version of Sentence (3)?
   A. NO CHANGE
   B. The deep sea is second only to space exploration.
   C. Second only to space exploration is traveling to the deep sea.
   D. Second to space exploration is the deep sea, and nothing after.
   E. Second only to space exploration in difficulty is exploring the deep sea.
24. Which is the best version of the underlined portion of Sentence (4)?
   A. NO CHANGE
   B. terribly inhospitable to human exploration
   C. terrible and inhospitable to human exploration
   D. terrible inhospitable to exploration by humans
   E. terrible inhospitably to human exploration

25. The author would like to add a transitional sentence after Sentence (4). Which of the following is best?
   A. For example, vessels made for deep sea exploration must be made to withstand very high pressures.
   B. Space exploration leaves little to no margin for error.
   C. The epipelagic layer is home to almost all of the marine life, vastly disproportionate to its volume of the ocean.
   D. Deep sea exploration can only be conducted by vessels such as bathyscaphes, which are built to withstand the conditions.

26. Which is the best version of the underlined portion of Sentence (5)?
   A. NO CHANGE
   B. each ten meters deeper
   C. every ten meters deep
   D. every ten meters deeper you guy
   E. with every ten meters of depth

27. Which is the best version of Sentence (6)?
   A. NO CHANGE
   B. Not mentioning the darkness and extreme cold in the deeper layers of the sea.
   C. Aside from having higher pressure, the deeper layers of the sea are unlit and extremely cold.
   D. The deeper layers of the sea are extremely cold and dark.
   E. Not to mention the pressure in addition to the darkness and extreme cold of the deeper layers of the sea.

28. Which is the best version of the underlined portion of Sentence (7)?
  - A. NO CHANGE
  - B. the same decade in which humans landed on the Moon
  - C. the same decade that humans were landing on the Moon
  - D. at the same time that humans landed on the Moon
  - E. the same decade as the Moon landing

29. Which is the best version of the underlined portion of Sentence (8)?
  - A. NO CHANGE
  - B. designing, building, and piloting the bathyscaphe *Trieste*
  - C. designed, built, and piloted the bathyscaphe *Trieste*
  - D. designs, builds, and pilots the bathyscaphe *Trieste*
  - E. designed, built, and is piloting the bathyscaphe *Trieste*

30. Which is the best version of the underlined portion of Sentence (9)?
  - A. NO CHANGE
  - B. designed to withstand an intense pressure
  - C. designed withstanding the intensity of pressure
  - D. withstanding the intensity of pressure by design
  - E. with the intensity of pressure taken into design

31. How should the underlined portion of Sentence (10) be edited to be less redundant?
  - A. NO CHANGE
  - B. which is the deepest known point of the ocean being around 11,000 meters deep
  - C. which, having a depth of around 11,000 meters, is the deepest known point of the ocean
  - D. which at around 11,000 meters below sea level is the deepest known point of the ocean
  - E. which at around 11,000 meters deep is the deepest known point of the ocean

32. The inclusion of Sentence (11) serves which purpose in the passage?
  - A. It further illustrates how deep the *Trieste* traveled.
  - B. It explains how the *Trieste* helped us learn more about the natural world.
  - C. It gives an example of the extreme conditions faced by the *Trieste*.
  - D. It gives more information about the epipelagic layer.
  - E. It does not serve a purpose and should be edited out.

33. Which is the best version of the underlined portion of Sentence (12)?

A. NO CHANGE
B. They used high-powered lights
C. The researchers used high-powered lights
D. They were able to use high-powered lights
E. The researchers were using high-powered lights

34. Which of the following would be a good edit to make to the second paragraph?
   A. Add a sentence after Sentence (11) giving more information about how the *Trieste* contributed to scientific understanding.
   B. Add a sentence after Sentence (7) giving more context about the Moon landing in the 1960s.
   C. Add a sentence after Sentence (8) explaining from which countries the research team members were.
   D. Remove Sentence (9).
   E. Add a sentence after Sentence (11) explaining how the lights were able to work in such a high-pressure environment.

For questions 35 - 40, select the best answer choice to replace the underlined portion of each sentence while keeping the original meaning of the sentence.

35. Whatever you do, <u>make sure that you're never without</u> a photo identification card when you're traveling outside of the county.
   A. make sure that you're never without
   B. make sure you're without
   C. don't never be without
   D. being without
   E. never being without

36. <u>The writer's consistent use of rhetorical questions, which are questions designed to elicit thought but not necessarily a response from the reader.</u>
   A. The writer's consistent use of rhetorical questions, which are questions designed to elicit thought but not necessarily a response from the reader.
   B. The writer consistently uses of rhetorical questions, which are questions designed to elicit thought but not necessarily a response from the reader.
   C. The writer's consistent use of rhetorical questions are questions designed to elicit thought but not necessarily a response from the reader.
   D. The writer consistently is making use of rhetorical questions, which are questions designed to elicit thought but not necessarily a response from the reader.

E. The use of rhetorical questions consistently by the writer, which are questions designed to elicit thought but not necessarily a response from the reader.

37. Beloved by all, <u>the fact that the committee decided to paint over that mural on 3rd Street is a travesty</u>.

    A. the fact that the committee decided to paint over that mural on 3rd Street is a travesty
    B. the committee cannot decide to paint over that mural on 3rd Street
    C. that mural on 3rd Street was shockingly condemned to be painted over by the committee
    D. it is a travesty that the committee condemned the mural on 3rd Street to be painted over
    E. painting over the mural on 3rd Street by the committee is a travesty

38. The product of a classical dance training and an immersion in contemporary modern theory, <u>the new exhibition at the ballet center shattering barriers</u>.

    F. the new exhibition at the ballet center shattering barriers
    G. shattering barriers is the new exhibition at the ballet center
    H. the exhibition which is new at the ballet center is shattering barriers
    I. the new exhibition at the ballet center shatters barriers
    J. the new ballet center exhibition is shatters barriers

39. Due to the fare hikes, <u>which go into effect on Monday</u>, many subway commuters are now looking into alternate forms of transportation.

    A. which go into effect on Monday
    B. going into effect on Monday
    C. which on Monday will go into effect
    D. into effect on Monday
    E. which going into effect on Monday

40. Although in the past some chemists and physicists believed that matter was evenly distributed throughout an atom, <u>we now knew that in fact it is densely compacted in the nucleus</u>.

    A. we now knew that in fact it is densely compacted in the nucleus
    B. we now knew that in fact it was densely compacted in the nucleus
    C. we now know that it is densely compacted in the nucleus
    D. in fact it was densely compacted in the nucleus
    E. in fact it is dense compacted in the nucleus

Reading/English/Language Arts – Answers

Question	Answer	Question	Answer	Question	Answer	Question	Answer
1	A	11	C	21	B	31	D
2	E	12	E	22	D	32	B
3	D	13	D	23	E	33	C
4	A	14	D	24	B	34	A
5	E	15	E	25	A	35	A
6	C	16	A	26	E	36	B
7	D	17	D	27	C	37	C
8	B	18	C	28	A	38	D
9	B	19	E	29	C	39	A
10	D	20	C	30	A	40	C

Made in the USA
Lexington, KY
02 January 2014